DISCOVERING DINOSAURS
MIGHTY GIANTS

MICHAEL BENTON

© 2006 Alligator Books Limited

Author: Professor Michael Benton BSc, PhD
Illustrator: John Sibbick

Published by Alligator Books Limited
Gadd House, Arcadia Avenue
London N3 2JU

Printed in China

CONTENTS

EARTH'S LARGEST BEASTS

Dinosaurs are famous for being big. The biggest, such as _Brachiosaurus_ or _Diplodocus_, were ten times the size of an elephant – the biggest land animal today.

The largest complete skeleton found is of _Brachiosaurus_. It measured 22 metres long and 12 metres tall – about as high as a tall tree. Bones found in the United States show that there may have been dinosaurs called _Supersaurus_ and _Ultrasaurus_. These creatures would have been a third larger than _Brachiosaurus_, making them the biggest animals ever to have lived on Earth. By contrast, the smallest dinosaurs were about the same size as a chicken.

All dinosaurs belonged to a group of animals called reptiles. Reptiles have a backbone and scaly, waterproof skin. Most of them lay eggs. Today, reptiles include lizards, snakes, tortoises and crocodiles. Unlike crocodiles, which have short, sprawling legs and live in water, dinosaurs walked on upright, thick legs and lived on land.

No one has ever seen a living dinosaur. Scientists call the dinosaur age the Mesozoic Era. Different dinosaurs lived at different times. The biggest dinosaurs appeared around 200 to 150 million years ago.

Muttaburrasaurus

Camptosaurus

Iguanodon

HOW DO I SAY THAT?

- **MESOZOIC**
  MESS-OH-ZOH-IK
- **CRETACEOUS**
  KRET-AY-SHUSS
- **JURASSIC**
  JOO-RASS-IK
- **TRIASSIC**
  TRY-ASS-IK

Theropods

A group of dinosaurs that included all huge, two-legged meat-eaters. *Allosaurus* had razor-sharp teeth. *Ceratosaurus* is famous for the unusual 'horns' on its face.

Ouranosaurus

Ceratosaurus

Ornithopods

These were plant-eaters. While not the biggest dinosaurs, the largest ornithopods were known for their big heads, horse-like snouts, strong hind legs and broad feet that supported their bulk. The four iguanodontids here had flat, hoof-like claws, making them more suited to walking than grasping objects.

Allosaurus

Sauropods

Plant-eating dinosaurs sauropods had gigantic barrel-shaped bodies, pillar-like legs and massive feet. They include *Apatosaurus* and *Diplodocus*.

Apatosaurus

FACTFILE: THE DINOSAUR AGE

- The Mesozoic Era lasted from 250 to 65 million years ago. Mesozoic means 'middle life'.

- The Cretaceous Period lasted from 150 to 65 million years ago. Cretaceous comes from the Latin *creta* ('chalk').

- The Jurassic Period lasted from 205 to 150 million years ago. It was named after the Jura Mountains, France.

- The Triassic Period lasted from 250 to 200 million years ago. Triassic means 'three-part'.

GIANT REPTILES

Why were some dinosaurs so big? Large animals have a lot of advantages. A big carnivore can kill almost anything, so it will never go hungry. A huge herbivore can be so big that no meat-eater can attack it – think of a lion trying to eat an elephant. Big animals can cover long distances in search of food. However, large animals have to eat a lot. Their weight can put a strain on their bones, causing health problems such as arthritis.

The longest dinosaur known was *Diplodocus*. Its skeleton measured 27 metres in length. Giants like *Diplodocus* weighed about 50 tonnes. It had four legs, so each leg had to support more than 10 tonnes. Its backbone was like the flat roadway of a bridge, slung between the hip girdle and the shoulder girdle. It needed strong muscles and ligaments just to support its huge weight. Giant dinosaurs could not move fast. If *Diplodocus* tried to gallop it would have broken its legs.

Hand bones

Hind foot bones

Big bones
Sauropods such as Brachiosaurus *had massive hands and feet to support their huge weight. The bones are enormous – each toe bone is as big as your thigh bone!*

Giant bridges
Sauropods are built like suspension bridges. A suspension bridge uses massive steel cables to hold up the flat road surface over which cars and people cross. In a sauropod, the backbone, long neck and tail, were held up by huge cable-like muscles and tendons that stretched along the back.

DINO DICTIONARY

● **Carnivore:** an animal that feeds on meat and flesh

● **Herbivore:** an animal that feeds on plants

Tailing off
The sauropod tail was long and whip-like. It was made up of many very small vertebrae.

Strong tails
Spines above and below the tail vertebrae (segments of the backbone) helped the muscles whip the tail up and down and from side to side.

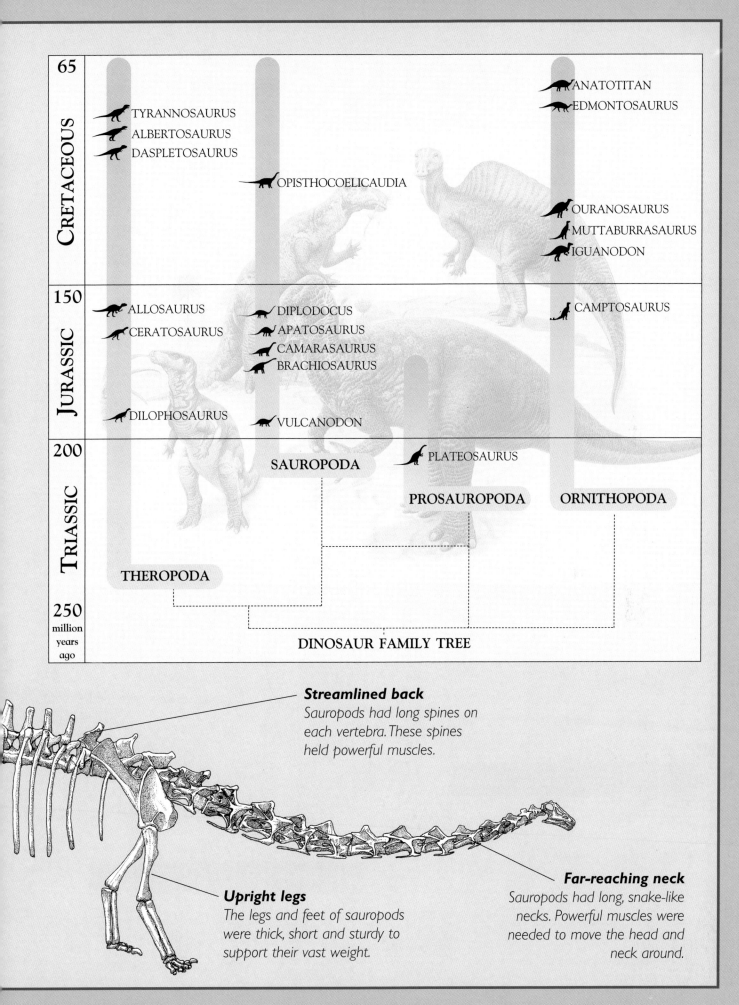

65			ANATOTITAN
			EDMONTOSAURUS
C	TYRANNOSAURUS		
R	ALBERTOSAURUS		
E	DASPLETOSAURUS		
T		OPISTHOCOELICAUDIA	OURANOSAURUS
A			MUTTABURRASAURUS
C			IGUANODON
E			
O			
U			
S			

CRETACEOUS

65
CRETACEOUS
TYRANNOSAURUS
ALBERTOSAURUS
DASPLETOSAURUS
ANATOTITAN
EDMONTOSAURUS
OPISTHOCOELICAUDIA
OURANOSAURUS
MUTTABURRASAURUS
IGUANODON

150
JURASSIC
ALLOSAURUS
CERATOSAURUS
DIPLODOCUS
APATOSAURUS
CAMARASAURUS
BRACHIOSAURUS
CAMPTOSAURUS
DILOPHOSAURUS
VULCANODON

200
TRIASSIC
SAUROPODA
PLATEOSAURUS
PROSAUROPODA
ORNITHOPODA
THEROPODA

250
million
years
ago

DINOSAUR FAMILY TREE

Streamlined back
*Sauropods had long spines on
each vertebra. These spines
held powerful muscles.*

Upright legs
*The legs and feet of sauropods
were thick, short and sturdy to
support their vast weight.*

Far-reaching neck
*Sauropods had long, snake-like
necks. Powerful muscles were
needed to move the head and
neck around.*

TERRIFYING T.REX

With a mouthful of razor-sharp teeth, each the size of a banana, *Tyrannosaurus rex* is famous for being a fearsome predator.

Was *Tyrannosaurus rex* a hunter that chased its prey at high speed, or was it a meat-eating scavenger? Fossil footprints give us clues about the speed and weight of a dinosaur. *T. rex* may have fed off slow-moving dinosaurs as well as dead animals. Some paleontologists (scientists who study fossils) believe that because *T. rex* was so heavy, it would not have been able to run much faster than you can. Fossil footprints made by *Tyrannosaurus* show that it could have outrun a rhinoceros, perhaps reaching 48 kilometres per hour. *T. rex* weighed as much as two elephants. This load would have put a lot of stress on its two leg bones. If the dinosaur tripped, it could never get up again.

Tail
When it ran, T. rex raised its tail high off the ground as a counter-balance.

Skull
T. rex had a huge head with deep, powerful jaws.

Feet
T. rex stood on two massive feet. It had a large claw at the end of each of its toes. A tiny fourth toe stuck out behind, but it did not reach the ground.

WHERE DID THEY LIVE?

Tyrannosaurus rex

HOW DO I SAY THAT?

TYRANNOSAURUS
TIE-RAN-OH-SAW-RUS

8

FACTFILE: TYRANNOSAURUS

- Lived: 75 to 65 million years ago
- Group: Theropoda
- Size: 14 m long, 6 m tall
- Weight: 6 to 7 tonnes
- Discovery: 1902, Montana, USA
- Diet: Carnivore
- Special features: huge teeth, tiny arms
- Name means: 'tyrant reptile'

Tyrannosaurus rex

Monster munch

Tyrannosaurus *was twice as tall as an elephant and could have picked you up in its jaws. It fed by holding down prey with one foot and tearing the flesh into strips with its strong jaws. It is hard to see how* T. rex *used its tiny arms. They did not even reach its mouth!*

TYRANT HUNTERS

Tyrannosaurids, such as *Albertosaurus* and *Daspletosaurus*, were relatives of *T. rex*. Being smaller, they moved much faster than most other theropods.

Like *T. rex*, *Albertosaurus* had only two fingers on its short arms. But *Albertosaurus* was probably more of an active hunter than *T. rex*. It would have killed its prey either by biting a lump of flesh from the neck, or by a powerful kick with its foot.

Daspletosaurus lived at the same time as *Albertosaurus*. Scientists cannot explain how two different tyrannosaurids, were able to live without competing for the same food. *Daspletosaurus* had a heavier head and larger teeth than *Albertosaurus*, so perhaps it hunted different animals. Both were big enough to fight with faster dinosaurs, such as the duckbill hadrosaurs.

Powerful jaws
Daspletosaurus *may have killed its prey by snapping its jaws into the flanks of an animal, and leaving it to bleed to death.*

HOW DO I SAY THAT?

⬤ **ALBERTOSAURUS**
AL-<u>BERT</u>-OH-<u>SAW</u>-RUS

⬤ **DASPLETOSAURUS**
DASS-<u>PLEET</u>-OH-<u>SAW</u>-RUS

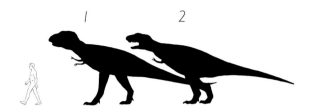

1. Daspletosaurus   2. Albertosaurus

Moving in on the kill

Like many meat-eating animals today, Albertosaurus and other tyrannosaurids were probably attracted by the smell of blood and may have fought over a kill.

FACTFILE: ALBERTOSAURUS

⬤ Lived: 75 to 65 million years ago

⬤ Group: Theropoda

⬤ Size: 9 m long

⬤ Weight: 2 to 3 tonnes

⬤ Discovery: 1892, Alberta, Canada

⬤ Diet: Carnivore

⬤ Special features: powerful legs, tiny arms

⬤ Name means: 'Alberta reptile'

11

JURASSIC KILLERS

The first predators had huge heads, powerful jaws and ferocious teeth – which they used to sink into the flesh of other dinosaurs they hunted.

The dinosaur age is often linked to the word 'Jurassic'. This refers to the period of time when large, meat-eating theropods appeared – about 195 million years ago. The best-known Jurassic theropod was *Allosaurus*. Its powerful teeth could tear the flesh of its prey into large chunks. *Ceratosaurus* lived at the same time as *Allosaurus*, but it was half the size and fed on much smaller prey. *Ceratosaurus*, meaning 'horned reptile', had odd-looking bumps on its skull that probably made it look more frightening. *Dilophosaurus* lived earlier in the Jurassic Period. It is famous for a pair of crests on top of its head. The crests looked like two halves of a dinner plate set up on end.

1. Ceratosaurus 2. Dilophosaurus
3. Allosaurus

Dilophosaurus

Ceratosaurus

HOW DO I SAY THAT?

● **ALLOSAURUS**
AL-OH-SAW-RUS

● **CERATOSAURUS**
SEE-RAT-OH-SAW-RUS

○ **DILOPHOSAURUS**
DIE-LOW-FOE-SAW-RUS

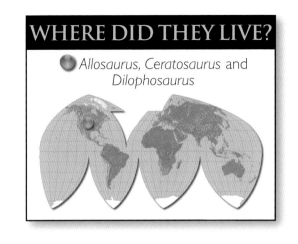

- Lived: 160 to 150 million years ago
- Group: Theropoda
- Size: 12 m long
- Weight: 4 to 5 tonnes
- Discovery: 1877, Colorado, USA
- Diet: Carnivore
- Special features: massive skull, powerful hands
- Name means: 'other reptile'

Fossil find

When 5000 Allosaurus bones were found in a quarry in Utah, USA, this large meat-eater became the best-known Jurassic theropod. It had sharp teeth and strong hands, each with three clawed fingers. It killed its prey by clamping its jaws around the animal's neck.

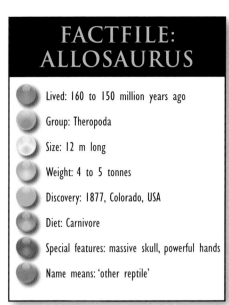

Allosaurus

THEROPODS

The first theropods had long arms and strong hands, with five fingers. They may have used the fingers seize and hold down its prey. Dinosaurs that came later, such as *Tyrannosaurus*, had short arms with two fingers, and short, strong thigh bones. This means that these later theropods may have been good runners. Theropods had blade-like, jagged teeth that curved into the mouth. Once the theropod sunk its jaws into its victim's flesh, the prey could not escape.

Theropods may have hunted in packs. Big predators, such as *Tyrannosaurus* and *Allosaurus,* probably hunted alone. They chased their prey, wrestling it to the ground and killed it by biting its neck. This is how lions and tigers hunt today. Large theropods probably hunted by stealth – staying very still until a plant-eater came near or creeping slowly through the trees and bushes until they were within striking distance. Then, with a quick leap, they would capture their prey!

Run for your life!
T. rex had massive jaws and a powerful neck. This suggests that the dinosaur hunted by charging at its prey, such as the duckbill above, and hitting it hard. T. rex would then snap shut its huge jaws around the animal's neck.

Ceratosaurs
This illustration of a Ceratosaurus skeleton clearly shows the dinosaur's powerful legs and backbone.

THE THEROPODS:

- *Albertosaurus*
- *Ceratosaurus*
- *Dilophosaurus*
- *Allosaurus*
- *Daspletosaurus*
- *Tyrannosaurus*

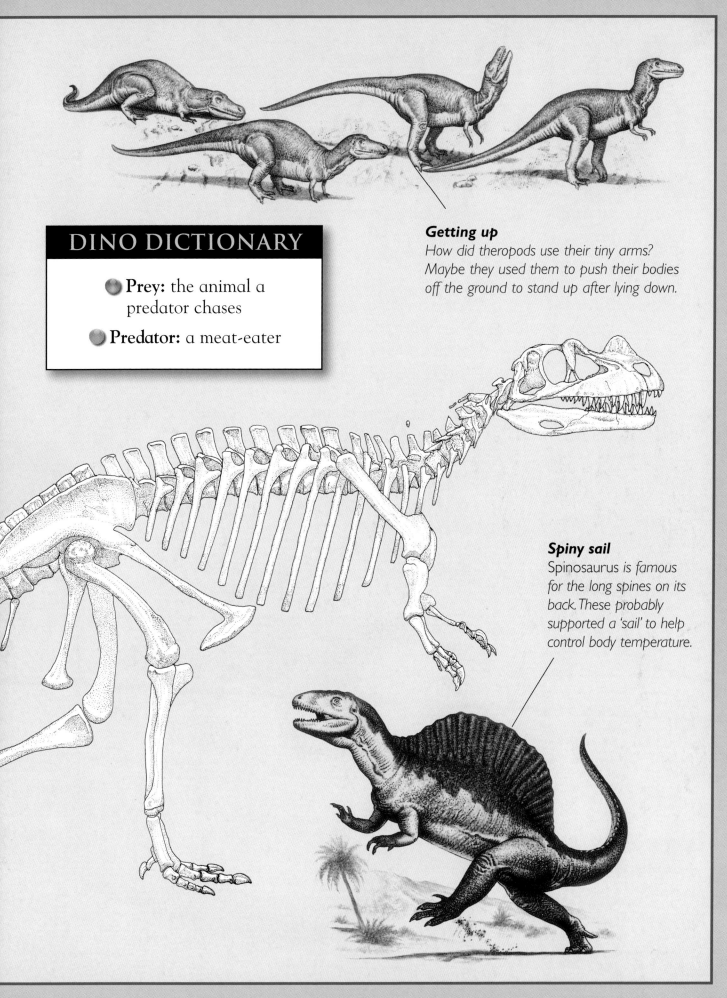

DINO DICTIONARY

● **Prey:** the animal a predator chases

● **Predator:** a meat-eater

Getting up
How did theropods use their tiny arms? Maybe they used them to push their bodies off the ground to stand up after lying down.

Spiny sail
Spinosaurus is famous for the long spines on its back. These probably supported a 'sail' to help control body temperature.

THE FIRST PLANT-EATERS

The true giants of the dinosaur age – the sauropods – evolved from medium-sized prosauropods such as *Plateosaurus*.

The first dinosaurs were human-sized, meat-eating reptiles. They appeared in the middle of the Triassic Period, around 230 million years ago. Then came the bigger, plant-eating 'early sauropods', known as the prosauropods. Later, prosauropods evolved (developed over a long time) into the gigantic sauropods, such as *Diplodocus* and *Apatosaurus,* of the Jurassic Period.

The first large prosauropod was *Plateosaurus.* This dinosaur was eight metres long. It was the largest land animal that had ever existed. Like all prosauropods, *Plateosaurus* walked on four legs, but it was light enough to stand easily or run on two legs. When standing, *Plateosaurus* used its huge hands, armed with claws, to pull tree branches to its mouth. Other large prosauropods included *Massospondylus* in South America and *Lufengosaurus* in Asia. Sauropods were heavier and four-footed. They were similar to *Plateosaurus* with their long, slender bodies, whip-like tails, enormously long necks and thin, pencil-shaped teeth.

HOW DO I SAY THAT?

● PLATEOSAURUS
PLAT-EE-OH-SAW-RUS

Armed and dangerous!

Plateosaurus *had huge, powerful hands armed with long claws. The thumb was very strong and carried the largest claw.*

Plateosaurus

FACTFILE: PLATEOSAURUS

- Lived: 220 to 205 million years ago
- Group: Prosauropoda
- Size: 6 to 8 m long
- Weight: 4 to 6 tonnes
- Discovery: 1837, Germany
- Diet: Herbivore
- Special features: powerful hands, walks on two or four legs
- Name means: 'flat reptile'

Hands up!

As a plant-eater, Plateosaurus *needed special hands that could support its weight, grasp tree branches and fight off predators.*

WHERE DID THEY LIVE?

● *Plateosaurus* ● Other prosauropods

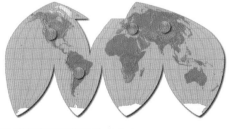

Quick getaway

Plateosaurus *fed close to the ground or high up in the trees. It moved around on all fours. When alarmed, it would rear up and run away on its hind legs.*

CLASSIC GIANTS

The biggest dinosaurs of all time were the sauropods. *Diplodocus* **and** *Apatosaurus* **were the best known, with their long, snake-like necks.**

Diplodocus is the longest sauropod that ever existed, measuring 27 metres from snout to tail. Why did sauropods have such long necks? It was probably to help them feed with less effort. Instead of wandering about, *Diplodocus* stood still and swept its head from side to side over a wide area of plants. When you weigh 30 tonnes, this takes much less energy than moving around all the time.

When fossils of *Apatosaurus* bones were first found, the skeleton had no head. It was suspected that the creature was the short-snouted *Camarasaurus*. Later study showed that it was *Apatosaurus* – a close relative of *Diplodocus* with a much a longer head.

On the receiving end
Some scientists believe that the sauropods used their enormously long tails to hit their enemies.

HOW DO I SAY THAT?

● APATOSAURUS
AH-PAT-OH-SAW-RUS
● DIPLODOCUS
DIP-LOD-O-KUS

1. Apatosaurus 2. Diplodocus

FACTFILE: APATOSAURUS

- Lived: 160 to 150 million years ago
- Group: Sauropoda
- Size: 21 m long
- Weight: 30 tonnes
- Discovery: 1877, Colorado, USA
- Diet: Herbivore
- Special features: long neck, heavy body
- Name means: 'deceptive reptile'

Vegetarian life

Plant-eating dinosaurs had to eat a lot to stay healthy. Grass did not appear on Earth until after the dinosaurs had become extinct. *Apatosaurus* might have fed on tough plants called ferns. It stripped the leaves off with its blunt, pencil-like teeth. *Apatosaurus* probably had stones inside its stomach to help grind up the plants.

WHERE DID THEY LIVE?

Apatosaurus and *Diplodocus*

19

THE BIGGEST EVER?

Most records of huge dinosaurs are based on limited fossil evidence – a giant leg bone or other parts of a monster skeleton. But few people doubt the enormity of *Brachiosaurus*.

Complete skeletons of *Brachiosaurus* were found in Tanzania, Africa, and they are huge. One of the skeletons is on display at the Humboldt Museum in Berlin, Germany, where it towers four floors high. With its long neck and enormous front legs, *Brachiosaurus* reached high above any other dinosaur to crop leaves from the tallest trees.

    Camarasaurus was much smaller than *Brachiosaurus*. At 18 metres long, however, it was still the size of six elephants! The head of *Camarasaurus* had a short snout. The jaws were lined with sharp teeth to chew on tough vegetation. As with *Brachiosaurus* and all the giant, plant-eating dinosaurs, *Camarasaurus* had front legs that were shorter than the back legs. Its feet were heavily padded – to absorb the shock of impact from the creature's huge weight on the ground.

HOW DO I SAY THAT?

● **BRACHIOSAURUS**
BRAK-EE-OH-SAW-RUS

● **CAMARASAURUS**
KAM-AH-RA-SAW-RUS

Head first
Brachiosaurus *is the tallest known dinosaur. For such a mountain of flesh and bone, the head of this creature might seem strangely small.*

Sharp teeth

Herbivore Brachiosaurus had sharp, peg-like teeth for nibbling plants.

1. *Camarasaurus* 2. *Brachiosaurus*

FACTFILE: BRACHIOSAURUS

Lived: 160-150 million years ago

Group: Sauropoda

Size: 22.5 m long, 12 m tall

Weight: 50 tonnes

Discovery: 1900, Colorado, USA

Diet: Herbivore

Special features: the tallest dinosaur, crest over eyes

Name means: 'arm reptile'

WHERE DID THEY LIVE?

Brachiosaurus and Camarasaurus

Brachiosaurus

Short differences

Camarasaurus was *smaller than* Brachiosaurus. *It had a shorter neck and front legs.*

BODY DEFENCES

The sauropods were one of the longest-living family of dinosaurs. A range of body defences helped them to survive the predators of the Late Jurassic Period.

One of the first sauropods of the Early Jurassic was *Vulcanodon* from Zimbabwe, Africa. It was smaller than most sauropods, but at 6.5 metres long, it was big enough to have straight pillar-like legs to support its body. Most of the toes ended in short 'hooves', except for the thumb claw, which was long and sharp. Perhaps this claw was used as a form of defence to fight off predators.

By the end of the dinosaur age in the Late Cretaceous period, most of the sauropods were armoured with plates. These would have made it difficult for meat-eating dinosaurs to hunt them for food. *Saltasaurus,* from South America, had plates set in its skin. Large and small bony plates joined up to form a strong chain mail. *Opisthocoelicaudia,* from China, had an unusually strong tail. This helped the dinosaur prop itself on two legs. It may have also been used as a defending 'weapon'.

HOW DO I SAY THAT?

● OPISTHOCOELICAUDIA
OH-PISS-THO-SEE-LI-COW-DEE-AH

● SALTASAURUS
SAL-TA-SAW-RUS

● VULCANODON
VUL-KAY-NO-DON

Vulcanodon
Little is known about Vulcanodon, *because only one incomplete skeleton has been found. The name means 'volcano tooth' – the first fossil was found close to some ancient volcanic lavas.*

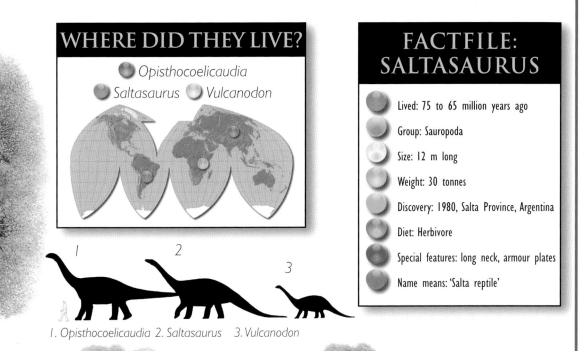

WHERE DID THEY LIVE?

- Opisthocoelicaudia
- Saltasaurus
- Vulcanodon

1   2

3

1. Opisthocoelicaudia 2. Saltasaurus   3. Vulcanodon

FACTFILE: SALTASAURUS

- Lived: 75 to 65 million years ago
- Group: Sauropoda
- Size: 12 m long
- Weight: 30 tonnes
- Discovery: 1980, Salta Province, Argentina
- Diet: Herbivore
- Special features: long neck, armour plates
- Name means: 'Salta reptile'

Tail props

Opisthocoelicaudia *had a strong, stiff tail. This dinosaur used its tail as a prop. It could reach high into the trees by rocking back on the tail and lifting its front quarters off the ground.*

Plate armour

Saltosaurus *is famous for its armour plates. This was probably a good defence against predators.*

SAUROPODS

When you look at a sauropod's skeleton, you can see that it is built for strength. The long neck and tail worked like the boom on a crane. In a large sauropod, the neck must have weighed about four tonnes, so it had to be strong. Powerful muscles and ligaments ran down the top of the neck. These could shorten to lift the neck up. The long whip-like tail could be raised and swung rapidly from side to side, probably to whack predators.

THE SAUROPODS:

- *Apatosaurus*
- *Brachiosaurus*
- *Camarasaurus*
- *Diplodocus*
- *Opisthocoelicaudia*
- *Plateosaurus*
- *Saltasaurus*
- *Vulcanodon*

Clawed-up sauropods

Paleontologists have been puzzled by the big thumb claws of the sauropods. It is thought that they were used to fight off predators. Apatosaurus may have reared up and threatened fearsome flesh-eaters such as Allosaurus.

Apatosaurus

Allosaurus

Strong tails

Spines above and below the tail vertebrae helped the muscles whip the tail up and down and from side to side.

Tailing off

The sauropod tail was long and whip-like. It was made up of many very small vertebrae.

Wonder of the world

A complete skeleton of Brachiosaurus has been put together from fossils collected in Africa around 1912. It can be seen in the Humboldt Museum in Berlin, Germany. The huge, powerful neck towers high into the exhibit hall, and people can walk under the dinosaur's belly.

DINO DICTIONARY

- **Paleontologist:** a scientist who studies fossils
- **Skeleton:** the bony framework that supports the body
- **Vertebra:** a small bone of the backbone

Far-reaching neck
Sauropods had long, snake-like necks. Powerful muscles were needed to move the neck and head around.

Streamlined back
Sauropods had long spines on each vertebra. These spines held powerful muscles.

Underwater swimmers?
This picture shows Brachiosaurus standing in deep water. Scientists used to think that sauropods lived underwater. In the same way that your body floats in water, scientists believed that water would have helped support the huge weight of these dinosaurs. Sauropods could have floated in lakes and fed on plants around the lake edge. The problem with this theory is that these dinosaurs could not have breathed in deep water. Their lungs would have been about five metres below the surface. At that depth, the water pressure would have squashed their lungs.

Sturdy legs
The legs and feet of sauropods were thick and short to support their vast weight.

25

TWO-LEGGED MONSTERS

These bird-footed runners attacked enemies with a vicious, dagger-like thumb claw.

The best-known ornithopod is *Iguanodon*. Its skeleton was one of the first ever to be found. *Iguanodon* stood and ran on its hind legs, but it could swing down on to its hands to feed on low-lying plants. *Iguanodon* had hooves on its feet and a mixture of hooves and claws on its hands.

The four ornithopods, shown together in this picture, lived in different parts of the world. *Iguanodon* is best known from fossil finds in Europe. *Ouranosaurus* lived in Africa and *Muttaburrasaurus* in Australia. *Camptosaurus*, an early ornithopod, came from North America.

HOW DO I SAY THAT?

● **CAMPTOSAURUS**
KAMP-TOE-SAW-RUS

● **IGUANODON**
IG-WAN-OH-DON

● **MUTTABURRASAURUS**
MUT-AH-BUR-AH-SAW-RUS

● **OURANOSAURUS**
OO-RAN-OH-SAW-RUS

Camptosaurus
*An early ornithopod
of the Late Jurassic.*

1. Camptosaurus
2. Ouranosaurus
3. Muttaburrasaurus
4. Iguanodon

Ouranosaurus
Famous for the sail running along its back and tail.

Muttaburrasaurus
An ornithopod with a bump on its snout.

Defending claw
The large thumb claw of the ornithopods is a bit of a mystery. Why would a peaceful plant-eater have had such a lethal weapon? It may have been used to scare off enemies or to attract a mate.

Iguanodon
A dinosaur with huge, three-toed feet. Each toe ended with a small hoof instead of a claw.

WHERE DID THEY LIVE?

Camptosaurus   Iguanodon
Muttaburrasaurus   Ouranosaurus

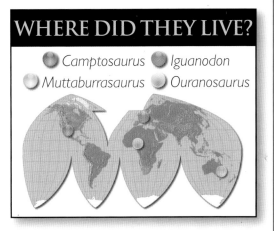

27

THE DUCKBILLS

Recognised by their unusual heads, these fast-running, plant-eating ornithopods appeared late in the dinosaur age.

Hadrosaurs are also called 'duckbills' because of their duck-shaped heads. Duckbills were so similar that their skeletons are almost impossible to tell apart. The main differences are in the shape of the head. *Anatotitan* had a long, low snout. *Bactrosaurus* had a short snout, while *Kritosaurus* had a low hump in front of the eyes.

Duckbills lived mainly in North America and Asia in huge herds made up of different species. They relied on speed to escape from predators. Although they would go on all fours to feed, they rose up on their powerful back legs to run. Their tails stuck out behind as a counterbalance.

Balloon-face
Kritosaurus *had a low crest over its snout. This may have been covered with loose skin. It could then be blown up like a balloon when the creature bellowed.*

HOW DO I SAY THAT?

● **ANATOTITAN**
AH-<u>NAT</u>-OH-<u>TEE</u>-TAN

● **BACTROSAURUS**
BAK-TRO-<u>SAW</u>-RUS

● **EDMONTOSAURUS**
ED-<u>MONT</u>-OH-<u>SAW</u>-RUS

● **KRITOSAURUS**
<u>KRIT</u>-OH-SAW-<u>RUS</u>

FACTFILE: EDMONTOSAURUS

- Lived: 75 to 65 million years ago
- Group: Ornithopoda
- Size: 10 to 13 m long
- Weight: 8 to 10 tonnes
- Discovery: 1892, Alberta, Canada
- Diet: Herbivore
- Special features: duck-like snout, hooves on hand
- Name means: 'Edmonton reptile'

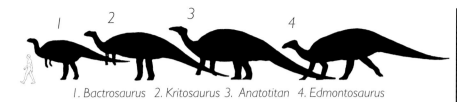

1. Bactrosaurus 2. Kritosaurus 3. Anatotitan 4. Edmontosaurus

WHERE DID THEY LIVE?

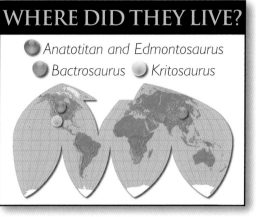

Anatotitan and Edmontosaurus

Bactrosaurus   Kritosaurus

Bactrosaurus
This is one of the ealiest hadrosaurs. It lived in Asia, so it would not have come across the three other North American dinosaurs.

Easy eating
Anatotitan shows its 'duckbill', which was used to gather plant food.

Edmontosaurus
One of the largest hadrosaurs, Edmontosaurus had hooved hands and feet, so that it could run on two or four legs.

29

ORNITHOPODS

Ornithopods had a mouthful of blunt teeth, which were perfect for grinding up plants. In fact, the duckbills had up to 300 teeth in each jaw, arranged in several rows. As the top row wore out the next row moved up to fill the gap.

Duckbills had large nostrils (the big openings at the front of the snout). This means that duckbills may have had a good sense of smell. They also may have been able to snort and bellow through their noses. The nose could have been used for signalling purposes, enabling the duckbill to produce distinctive calls. Some duckbills had such long noses, suggesting that they could have been used for feeding underwater. The nose could act as a snorkel so the creature could breathe while eating.

Hooves
Duckbills had small hooves on most of their fingers because the hands were used for walking.

 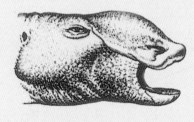

Bellowing snouts
Duckbill hadrosaurs such as Edmontosaurus *could bellow by inflating a balloon-like area of skin over their snouts.*

THE ORNITHOPODS:

- *Anatotitan*
- *Edmontosaurus*
- *Maiasaura*
- *Bactrosaurus*
- *Iguanodon*
- *Muttaburrasaurus*
- *Camptosaurus*
- *Kritosaurus*
- *Ouranosaurus*

Back

Ornithopods often had little strips of criss-crossed bone along the backbone. These structures started out as flesh, but turned to bone to strengthen the back as the dinosaur grew older.

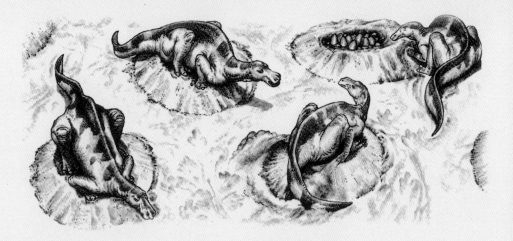

Parental care

Recent discoveries show that dinosaurs cared for their young. Maiasaura, a duckbill hadrosaur, is known as the 'good mother' dinosaur. Like all dinosaurs, it laid its eggs in shallow nests scooped out of the earth. Whole colonies of Maiasaura nests have been found, and there is evidence that the mothers laid their eggs, covered them, and then guarded the nests. Each female dinosaur in the colony would look after her eggs, keeping her distance from her neighbours. When the eggs hatched, the parents brought them soft plants to eat. This parental care continued until the young grew old enough to look after themselves.

Tail

Long, rib-like bones ran underneath the tail. These indicate that the ornithopods had powerful muscles in their tails.

Legs

Ornithopods had strong, pillar-like legs, which were designed for support and long spells of running. They needed these powerful legs so that they outrun their predators.

DINO DICTIONARY

● **Parental care:** the mother and father look after the young

31

INDEX